21 Spells Of Love

Apoorvaa Kulkarni

BookLeaf Publishing

India | USA | UK

Made with ❤ on the BookLeaf Publishing Platform
www.bookleafpub.in
www.bookleafpub.com

Dedication

To *Aai*, who embedded a dream into my soul—
We have to publish your poetry book.

To *Namrata*,
who blackmailed me with love until I believed—I am a
poetess.

To *Varun*,
who never let my art go unheard.

To my father, who named me a writer,
and to my brother, who reminded me of my worth.

To all who breathed life into these poems,
and to those who will live forever within them.

To Rumi, who wove poetry into my skin and bones,
until I could no longer tell where verse ended and I
began.

To love, to loss,
and to this beautiful, aching grey we all call life.

Preface

Love casts its spells upon us in all colours and forms.

Some lovers manage to find their fairy tales, while others only seek. They say love blinds us, but how can we resist these ever-lasting spells? What can one do when the definition of colours keeps changing in love, shifting like the very winds of the heart? For one, red might mean desire, for others it may ignite anger. These spells are shaped by the palettes of human emotions, ever-evolving and unpredictable.

This book is an attempt to unravel these spells, to dive deep through their layers and to awaken the forgotten, dusty corners of your heart. I hope to revisit the understanding of love and revive what has long been silenced.

21 Spells of Love takes you on a journey through the emotions that swirl around us, as love continues to cast its spells and pull us through its endless dance—onward and beyond. Each poem tells a story, a moment in which love's magic transports you to realms beyond the mundane, to cosmic spaces where time and place are bent. One cannot experience a spell without suffering

through another.

Love, in its most potent form, is always paradoxical. It can be so simple, yet when it strikes, it complicates everything. Perhaps it's because we often view love as a bond between two souls. When we love, we expect the other to love us back. Yet love knows no boundaries. People fight wars in love. It grants the sweetest nectars of heaven, and it drowns you into the depths of hell. Love can be a momentary experience. It can also last a lifetime. It might knock at your door in the still of midnight, it might also leave in broad daylight. Love defies gender, it defies age. Love is a force that transcends time and reality. Love keeps us united, love binds us too. No matter how many times you experience its magic, every time love casts a spell, each one always feels new. Love breaks through the opaque. Love heals the deepest wounds.

21 Spells of Love does not simply recount the many faces of love—it dares to reveal them, raw and unfiltered. It strips away the illusions we've clung to, ripping apart the veils we've used to hide from the truth. This is no mere journey—it is a reckoning, a confrontation with the forces that shape us. Love's spell does not only change the course of your heart, it fractures it. It shatters the walls you've built, pulling you into the deepest corners

of your soul, and forcing you to confront what lies there. In this moment, you are no longer who you were. After love's spell, you cannot go back. You are remade—transformed, broken, rebuilt. And in that breaking, you will find that you are not only more whole than you were before, but infinitely more alive.

Acknowledgements

First and foremost, I owe everything to love itself—the force that binds us all, in all its complex and ever-changing forms. Without love, there would be no poetry, no stories to tell, no magic to weave. It is the very essence of life, and through its many faces, I have been both humbled and transformed. Every word in this book is a spell cast by love itself.

To those who have crossed my path—those who have loved me, hurt me, healed me, and shown me the countless layers of the heart—thank you. You are the whispers in the pages, the pulse behind every line. Your stories, your quiet suffering, your laughter, and your joy have filled this book with meaning. It is through you that I have found my voice.

To my family: you have been my unwavering anchor and my safe haven. Your love has been the constant spell that kept me grounded and inspired. In times of doubt, your belief in me was the magic I clung to. Without you, these pages would not exist.

To my friends, who have been my mirrors, reflecting both the brightest and the darkest parts of me. You have offered your hearts without hesitation, and your support has been the shield against the storms of life. You have shown me that friendship is the truest form of love. Thank you for laughing with me, crying with me, and for always showing up when I needed you the most.

To my mentors, guides, and fellow poets—your wisdom has been the spark that ignited this journey. In your words, I found the courage to embrace my own voice. You have shown me that poetry is not just a craft, but a way of seeing the world, a way of being. Thank you for your generosity and your unflinching belief in the power of words.

A special mention to Rumi, whose words continue to light my path like a lantern in the dark. His understanding of love and the soul transcends time, and it is through his poetry that I first learned to hear the heartbeat of the universe. Rumi's spell continues to guide me, reminding me that love is both the question and the answer.

To Shiva and Sati, the eternal dance of destruction and creation, and the profound beauty found in the balance between the divine masculine and feminine. Their story has shown me that love is not always gentle—it is fierce, it is raw, and it is transformative. Their love is an embodiment of power, sacrifice, and transcendence.

To the world of Harry Potter, where magic is a part of everyday life, and love is the most potent force of all. I will ALWAYS be grateful to J.K Rowling for bringing to life all the characters who taught me that love's power is boundless, and that even in the darkest of times, love can heal, protect, and ultimately save us.

Finally, to you, the reader—thank you for opening this book and allowing these spells to find a home in your heart. Every word, every line, was written with you in mind. It is my hope that the magic contained here will stir something within you, whether it be joy, sorrow, or the quiet realization that love, in all its forms, is the one constant force that makes us human. May these poems speak to you as they have spoken to me.

With deep love, boundless gratitude, and infinite reverence,
Apoorvaa Kulkarni

Unraveling You...

- for those who became galaxies, just by loving too deeply

You hope to someday find someone,
but that hope feels more like a fantasy.
You know
(because you've read The Fault in Our Stars)
that the world is not a wish-granting factory.
But still, you hope for a fairy tale...

Yet every fairy tale comes with its own tragedy—
one you're utterly unprepared for.
And so, you fear.
When life starts taking you on the journey toward a
fairy tale,
you panic.
You stop.

You ask the stranger to stay away,
because if he comes too close,
you're afraid your fairy tale will end
before it can even begin.

So, you keep dreaming.
You dream about a future,
about having that love in your life
you've always longed for.
You dream about your fairy tale.

And then,
you meet this person—
the one who makes you believe your fairy tale has
begun.
You fall for the trap,
this ultimate delusion.
And your fairy tale?
It still seems as distant as the horizon.

Now, the land of your heart feels barren.
So much so that love itself seems like a wonderland.
And you are Alice.
You fantasize about a companion
to walk that barren land with you—
you desire the warmth of someone's presence.

And yet again,
you hope for a fairy tale.
This time,
you know they won't stay.

So, you hope only for a moment.
Forever feels forever away.

But then—
magic happens.
Love casts its spell yet again.
The fairy tale you once dreamt of—
you become a part of it.

Your need for connection—
the universe hears it.

You submerge into your fairy tale.
It no longer belongs to you.
It consumes you whole.

And then,
you experience love—
its beauty, its depth.
You start wishing again,
daydreaming again.

Maybe this time,
it won't be a delusion.

You experience a love so sacred,
you begin to worship it.
Every second, every minute,
of every single day—
love keeps eating you.

And then the buzz stops.
You feel one with the cosmos.
You feel parts of you healing
that you never realized were so heavily wounded.

And then—
you surrender.
You understand the universe works
in its own mysterious ways.
You let the magic enfold.
You take the passenger seat,
because you know—
the one driving is the ultimate reality.

With surrender comes awakening.
Where the physical boundaries of this world prick you,
you rise above them all.

You begin to wonder—
about a world away from it all,
where only love lasts,
even when everything else fades.

And then—chaos.
Utter, mad chaos.

You realize the love was sacred
because you are sacred.
That you could worship love
only because you are divine.
This is when you become the universe.

Loving someone becomes a curse you carry.
The universe within tells you—
their betrayal doesn't mean love
has lost its divinity.
Every fairy tale has its tragedy.
And your tragedy makes you weep.

You want love to heal your wounds...

But you finally accept—
love cannot.
Because you are love.
You are the magic enfolding.

The phoenix of your soul
rises from the ashes—
charred,
but still,
magnificent as ever.

You look back and realize
how much you've lost.
The loss feels too heavy,
too personal,
almost unbearable...

Your fairy tale succumbs to melancholy.
You curse the heavens
and bleed into hell.

The burden of becoming the universe—
it weighs on you.
And then, you realize—
it's just you.
All alone.
You almost had them.
But you don't.

And now you know—
you need to keep walking.

Abyss, hollow—no matter what.
Even when the horizon feels a distant dream,
the light at the end calls you,
lures you,
makes you crawl out of your pit.

The universe within rages a war.
The brave ones win.

And then—
love casts a lethal spell.
It wraps itself in grief,
knocks on your door,
and delivers posts filled with emptiness.

You know now—
to love never meant
to actually have a companion.
You know now—
to love is to experience the cosmos and its magic,
happening through you,
stardust surging through your blood.

And yet,
the spell of love lingers.
It lasts forever.

Through these memories—
you carry on.
You rise.
You evolve.
You die.
Yet still,
you live.

You keep on living
until you remember—
You are love.

The love within you
liberates your soul.
You dream of colors again.
You finally stop feeling dead.
You finally
have hope again.

It happens when
the universe within
makes you understand—

You are poetry.

You are the cosmos.
You are life.
And you are Love.

You are the fairy tale.
Everyone else—
they're just a part of it.

1. Hope

Let's meet at the centre,
at the crossroads,
where your world and mine intersect
symmetrically,
where life enfolds—
a magic land,
a wish-granting factory,
a fantasy,
a hope.

Why, you ask?

My love, it's got to be a magic land, if we meet!
How else could we ever achieve that feat?

In the whispers of time,
let us take our chance,
where laughter echoes
and our souls can dance,
where our hearts beat in one tune
and time suspends
like a mysterious rune.

Let's meet at the centre,
at the crossroads,
where your world and mine intersect
symmetrically,
and call it a date—
where the moon's bright and it's a starry night,
where dreams come true:
a magic land,
a wish-granting factory,
a fantasy,
a hope.

2. Fear

Don't come too close, stranger,
or you'll hear the screams and wails of my heart,
caused by the stampede of my thoughts.

Don't come too close, stranger,
or you'll notice a hint of agony in my sparkling eyes,
caused by the hurricane of my emotions.

Don't come too close, stranger,
or you'll see through the painted smile on my face—
at the barricade of my heart,
caused by the pain inflicted by my scars.

So stay.
Stay a bit away from me.

Because—
if you come too close,
I'm afraid
you won't come too close ever again.

So stay.
Stay a bit away from me.

3. Dream

I dream about a sunrise—
Waking up in bed beside you.

How the rays of the sun would fall upon your closed
eyes,
And they'd flicker for a moment...

How I'd want to be the first person you see
As you start a new day.

I dream about sharing a house with you—

How you'd start your day
With a cup of tea in one hand and a newspaper in the
other...

How we'd eat breakfast in bed,
And maybe take a shower together.

I dream about knowing everything about you someday—
How you'd pick a certain shirt on a particular day...

How you'd look as if, since I first saw you,
You haven't aged a day.

I dream about texting you during lunchtime from work—

Asking about your meetings,
Telling you about the pile of files on my desk...

How I'd imagine your face making all those expressions
As you tell me about a joke someone cracked earlier
today.

I dream about waiting for you to pick me up from work
in the evening—

How your face would change from tired
To suddenly relaxed and happy
At the sight of me waiting there for you...

How I'd sit beside you in the car and give a tired sigh;
How you'd take my hand into yours and plant a kiss on
it...

And how magically,
All my stress would disappear—just like that.

I dream about what we'd do while driving back toward
our home—
Maybe we'd halt at some random place in between,

Light two cigarettes and talk to each other,
Or just stand leaning against the bonnet of the car,
Looking into the blank...

How the silence wouldn't haunt us.

I dream about returning back home—

How we'd argue over who'd take a shower first...
How I'd pour us two glasses of wine
As we readied the dinner.

I dream about having dinner with you,
Watching a movie, a TV show,
Or a web series you're excited about...

How you'd listen to my rants about people at work,
How you'd complain about clients biting your head off...

How we'd plan a vacation,
And after discussing so many places,
Finally end up on Goa!

I dream about spending my weekends with you—

Waking up late in the morning,

Tossing about who'd make the tea,
Deciding whether to cook or order online...

How you'd hold onto me,
As if afraid that all of this would disappear someday.

I dream about fighting with you
Over what we'd watch on television—

A '90s rom-com or a superhero action movie...

How we could watch cricket together,
Shouting and cursing all the while...

How you'd swear if something didn't happen
The way you wanted it to.

I dream about going back to bed with you—

How I'd rest my head onto your chest
And feel your heartbeats...

How you'd wrap your arms tightly around me,
And all the worries of the world forgotten—

Just you and me—
In that moment of love, of bliss...

How we'd fall asleep together,
Anticipating a new day...

How we'd both think about the things we'd do
tomorrow,
Alone and together...

And how
in both our minds,
All our days would start and end
With us being in this bed—

Together.

Forever.

I dream.

4. Delusion

For you, it was a mere distraction.
For you, it was just an attraction.

But how could I know?

How could I know you did not feel a thing?
How could I know, for you, it meant nothing?

Tell me.

I fell for you with all my heart,
With the faith that you did the same.
But how could I know?
How could I know it was all in vain?

Tell me.

The way you looked at me—
As if I bore all the happiness in the world.
The way you caressed my hair,
As if, for you,
My happiness meant the world.

The way you used to smile
When I did crazy stuff.
The way you held my hand
When the times were tough.

But how could I know?
How could I know it was a bluff?

Tell me.

In the whole wide world,
I fell for you—
Like nothing and no one else mattered.
But—
Alas—
For me, it was love.
For you,
It was everything else—
But love.

Remember the rainy night
When you held an umbrella over us,
And looking into my eyes,
You said those precious words?

How time had stopped.
How the world had frozen.

From that moment on,
You felt like the only one
I would ever need.

But how could I know?

How could I know
That it was all an illusion?
How could I know
All you had was just confusion?

Tell me.

That moment
When we kissed for the first time ever—
Trust me,
I felt the possibility of a forever.

But—
How could I know it was just a kiss?
How ignorant I was!
It was such a bliss.

When I rested upon your shoulder
In moments of my need,

I should have known then—
All about your greed.

It felt like a beautiful dream
Amidst a chaotic reality.
And then,
You just left—
With a sudden finality.

The moments we shared,
The feelings I had—
With just a tick of the clock,
It all turned sad.

But how could I know
It was never meant to be?
How could I know
What you truly felt for me?

Tell me.

No matter how I wept.
No matter how close I kept.
No matter how hard I tried—
For you, it was never love.
I finally derived.

Even today, I think about you
On my brightest day.
Even today, your memory
Makes my day.

Even now,
I wonder how—
Why did it happen?
Where was the flaw?

Tell me.

In the end,
There is just one conclusion:
What I had was a daydream,
A delusion.

As for you, it was a mere distraction.
For you, it was just an attraction.

But how could I know?
Tell me.
For—
Oh baby,
I was so madly in love...

5. Fantasy

In the starry night along the barren land,
Let us wander around like Alice in Wonderland.

Hold my hand and take me through—
The roads are narrow, and the river is blue.

The cold wind blows when you come close,
And the dark night stares upon us.

The fire in your eyes brings us light,
But the touch of your lips feels like ice.

In the starry night along the barren land,
I feel warm when you hold my hand.

Let us walk, for the night is upon us.
Let us flee, for the darkness surrounds us.

Take me along—
With you, I belong,
Two wanderers seeking love all along.

Under the moonlight, when you gaze into my eyes,
I see the whole world, happy and bright.

In the starry night along the barren land,
Make love to me, for the night doesn't end.

When you wrap your arms around me,
I feel a fire burning inside me.

Beside you, I want to walk to the end,
In the hope that the night will never end.

All through the night, we keep walking ahead,
And all of a sudden, the skies start turning red.

I turn around and look into your eyes—
I see the light of the stars shining bright.

You come close and hold my hand,
And in that moment, we both understand:
All we wish is for the night to never end.

For in the starry night along the barren land,
I feel warm when you hold my hand.

Yet with the first rays of the sun
Begins a bright day.

And in the bright sunlight across the barren land,
We wander around like Alice in Wonderland.

The day passes by, and the North Star shines again.
Now we hope the night won't come again.

And yet the night comes, and we still stand,
Holding our hands, we cross the barren land.

For in the starry night along the barren land,
I feel warm when you hold my hand.

Let us wander around like Alice in Wonderland.

6. Desire

I need to get you out of my system—
Your intoxicating aroma,
The way your skin felt against mine...

The way my body responded to your touch,
How even the pain you gave brought pleasure.

I need you to intoxicate me
With the perfume of your body,
Pressed so closely against mine.
I need to feel one with you.

I need to kiss you like it's the end of the world.
I need us to move in harmony,
Our bodies composing music through rhythm.

I need you to hold me close.
I need you to hug me like it's the last time.
I need to shake, to twitch, to moan—
As you fill me with divinity.

I need to hear your whispered moans,
The way you softly say my name against my ear.

I need to connect with you—
Not just physically, but spiritually.
I need our souls to burn together
In orgasmic bliss.

I need you to look into my eyes,
Hold my gaze, and tell me you love me.
I need to see your eyes twinkle
As you look at me.

I need a thousand things...
Yet I need just one.

I need no one else.
I need only one—
You.

I need you to love me.
I need you to burn—
The way my body burns for you,
The way my heart beats for you.

I need you—
All of you, every inch of your body,
Every particle of your soul.

I need you to rescue me.

To hug me tight when the demons arrive.
To hold me close when the darkness rises.

I need you to stay—
Today and forever.
I need nothing and no one,
I just need you.

So stay...

Can you?

Will you?

If not—
I need to get you out of my system...

I need to get me into your system.
Just tell me how.

Just stay,
At least for a while.

Let me look at you long enough
To remember you for a lifetime.

Let me touch you long enough
To remember how your skin felt in my hand.

Let me hold you long enough
For your perfume to linger on me forever.

I need this.
If not you—
Then atleast this.

So stay.
If not forever,
At least for a while...

Can you?

Will you?

7. Promise

In a world full of ifs and buts,
I want to be the certainty you turn to
When life shows its true colors.

In a world full of blacks and whites,
I won't mind being the grey
To which you turn in your darkest times.

In a world full of rights and wrongs,
Let us do what our heart truly wants.

For, my love,
You are the rarest gem in a world of stone.
For, my love,
In a thousand voices, yours is the only one I've ever
known.

In a world full of sunrises and sunsets,
Let me rejoice in the sunshine of your smile.

Along with the moon and the stars,
What I love is the twinkle in your eyes.

For, my love,
You are the reason for my being.
For, my love,
You are my day and my dream.

In a world full of skies and seas,
I want to be the ground you need.

In a world full of dusks and dawns,
Let us be together all day long.

For, my love,
The future is bright.
For, my love,
With you, everything is always alright.

In a world full of days and nights,
Along with you, time always flies.

Along the oceans and amidst the clouds,
Let us travel where the horizon lies.

For, my love,
You are my heart's desire
For, my love,
You and I belong together.

When the days end and the nights descend,
By your side—
I will stand.

When the hopes are all gone,
And you are alone,
I promise to be with you all along.

For, my love,
You are the rarest gem in a world of stone.
For, my love,
In a thousand voices, yours is the only one I've ever
known.

For, my love,
You are my heart's desire.
For, my love,
You and I belong together—

Today, tomorrow, and forever.

8. Devotion

I look at the moon
as I lay on my bed...
wondering if
you are looking at it too.

I look at the moon
and I see you...
wondering if
you can see me too.

I look at the moon
and I miss you...
wondering if
you miss me too.

I look at the moon
as I lay on my bed...
imagining a beautiful life with you...
wondering if
you can imagine it too.

I look at you
as I look at the moon—
realizing

how much I love you...
wondering if
you could ever love me too.

I look at the moon
as I lay on my bed...
thinking about us...
about everything you ever said to me...
about what it meant
and what it didn't...
about all your words—
and how I interpreted them.

I look at the moon
and I see you—
smiling at me—
that wonderful smile of yours
that melts my heart
every time.

I look at the moon
and I feel your presence around me...
how you are with me
even when you aren't with me.

I look at the moon
and I see you

raising your eyebrows at me,
coming closer,
holding my hand
in yours.

I look at the moon
and I remember you.
I remember our love—
our numbered forever.

I look at the moon
and I see clearly
how I fell in love with you.

I look at the moon
and I see us—
together,
in the end,
leaving behind the abyss...
wondering
if this will ever be true.

I look at you
as I look at the moon...
wondering
how one could
not fall in love with you?

I look at the moon
and I think how beautiful you look—
when you lie beside me
with your messy hair—
realizing
how mess
never felt so good before.

I look at the moon
and I feel
a hurricane of emotions for you.
How far I've come
on this path of love...
There's so much chaos in my mind,
yet everything
ends with you.

Even the chaos
seems beautiful
when it includes you.

I look at the moon
and I hope
that you'll love me too...
if not forever,
maybe for a day,

for a minute,
for a second...

Wondering
if that day,
that minute,
that second—
would be my only moment
with you.

How I would live
an eternity
in that one moment.
How that one day,
one minute,
or one second—
would be
my forever.

I look at the moon
as I lay on my bed...
and I know—

I love you.
I have always loved you.
I will always love you.

No matter
how things turn out to be...

Because—
you are my forever.

9. Peace

With you,
there's no noise.

There's a voice.

When I walk around the world,
my energy reverberates
through the universe—
looking for a frequency
to match with,
looking for the unsettling noise
to stop.

But the buzz
never ends.

The hummmm
of all the energies around you—
none of them
resonate with yours.

And you walk through.
You keep traversing
through the energies,

through the frequencies,
until one fine day—

out of the blue,
out of all the buzz—

there's a hint of a voice.

A sound so familiar,
yet so unfamiliar—
because of how far
and long
you've journeyed.

And you halt
momentarily—

and that's it.

The buzz has stopped.
There's no noise anymore—
but a voice.

A voice
reaching out,
calling you
by your name.

Tuning into
your frequency,
resonating with
your energy,
your soul.

In you—
I find that voice.

The voice
that tunes the buzz off.
The voice
that pulls me
out of the white hole
I have no recollection
of ever entering.

All my life—
I kept getting sucked
deeper and deeper
into the black hole.

Are you a wormhole?
Are you a frequency?
Are you a soul?
Are you energy?

You're the voice.
You're the calling.
You're that light.

You're all of it—
except the buzz.

10. Surrender

The universe conspired
for our love to be slow.
It wanted us to meet,
to talk,
to hold each other.

We deserve an old-school love—
the universe planned it that way.

It allowed every moment in our lives
to unfold just so
that when the time was right,
we'd find each other—
as the exact versions of ourselves
we were always meant to be.

So that when we met,
we wouldn't dismiss each other.
We wouldn't fall back out.

A slight shift in timing,
and none of this would've felt the same.

The universe made us—
together—
like stars.

It let us live
the lives we were meant to lead,
only stepping in
at specific points
to mould us
into who we needed to be
when we entered each other's lives.

The point of our creation—
a single dot,
spreading in opposite directions
only to intersect
at the right moment in time.

And from here,
we live our lives together—
but not too together,
lest our love
fade
too soon.

So we walk,
side by side,

until death
makes us one again.

Unites us
as a single dot.
Reduces us
to that same beginning.

Circle of life.
Complete.

Yet we start again.

And so it shall go on,
indefinitely.

That's how we were meant to be.
That's how we were created.
That's how we shall end—
together.

A single dot.

That's how the universe conspired.
And that's how I know:

I am yours,
and you are mine—
before birth,
after death,
and through life.

11. Paranoia

When the sea bleeds,
and the mountains break down—
when the clouds cry,
and the skies start screaming—
meet me then.

Meet me then,
for if the world really ends,
I want to die
looking into your eyes.

Meet me then,
and hold me close—
so close
that it physically hurts.
Oh, but that sweet agony of love!

When the winds start pushing us,
and the dust pricks our eyes—
meet me then
and do not let go.
For wherever the world takes us,
I want to be with you
until the very end.

And if,
somehow,
miraculously,
we manage to survive—
promise to never leave my hand again.

Let's build a world together,
a world where no one
and nothing
can break us apart.

Let's build a world together,
where we never have to say goodbyes.

Let's build a world together,
and start living—
a life where you exist in mine,
and I exist in yours.

And if not,
then—

When the trees are burning,
and the cities are falling—
meet me then.

For if death is inevitable,
I want to greet the afterlife with you.

When the ground beneath us quivers,
and the earth consumes us whole—
do not let go.
As life slips away from us,
sail to paradise with me—

Where at least our souls
can be together.
For we deserve this, my love.
We really do.

So meet me then—
when the world's about to end.

12. Divinity

Your eyes...
They had that magic in them—
that small speck of bright white light
in which one could submerge
into an endless oblivion.

The way you looked at me—
as if I were the epitome of love and beauty in this world.
How you held me in your arms,
never looking away, not once...

The way your eyes bore deep into mine,
as if they were calling me in...
And I was pulled towards you,
towards the eyes that held the meaning of existence.

And so I took the leap,
submerging into them,
becoming one with you.

Oh, how you showed me
the core of my existence,
the meaning of my being.

And then—
you looked away,
leaving me naked,
sinking into the ocean of your eyes,
blinded by that white speck of light,
left at the bottom of the sea,
in an endlessness
that shook my entire being to its core.

I saw you looking at me
from far away—
as if daring me to come back.

How I ached.
How I longed for your touch.
How every inch of my skin
craved for your love.

But you just kept looking,
wondering how long before I gave up.

In that instant, I saw beyond your illusion—
beyond the eternity your eyes had promised me—
where lived a coward,
so afraid of love,
a cursed being beyond any hope of help.

And so I looked away,
blinking back into the chaos
that was my home.

In that moment,
I found my divinity.

How sacred my heart was.

Wow.

Chaos never felt so soothing before.

13. Betrayal

As I was living in my punctured oblivion,
You came to me—
Fuelled with emotions.

One look at you,
And I jumped with joy,
For you had finally come to me—
In an attempt to heal
All the unspoken wounds...
Or so I assumed.

Little did I know,
You carried matchsticks
Full of lies
In your back pocket.

And the moment I let my guard down,
Giving you a peek
Into the vulnerability I hid within myself—

You ignited those matchsticks
With strips of your shamelessness,
And you set me on fire.

Golden flames
Of chaos and betrayal
Wrapped my entire being.

As I looked at you
Through the flames—
My soul burning
Faster than my body ever could—
I saw no regret.
I saw no guilt.
Only a wicked sense of righteousness.

I wailed and cried,
Shouted and begged
For you to stop the madness,
To pour down on me
Buckets full of apologies.

Alas!

I kept writhing and screaming,
Caught in the wildfire
Of lies and chaos,
Hurt and betrayal—
Desperately searching
For a lake of emotion in your eyes.

I never found any.

My skin became bones,
And bones became ashes.
All that remained was my soul—
Longing to be saved
From the eternal cage
Of hatred and anger.

Longing
For the pain to stop.
For you to stop it
For me.

You never did.

Not even a shred of empathy
As my soul searched yours
One last time
Before letting you go
Forever.

In the end...

Even as I walked
The path toward my salvation,

The fumes of the consequences of your lies
Lingered on.

The smoke of lost hope
Suffocating everyone
We held dearly.

Everyone—
But you.

14. Acceptance

Loving you
is like trying
to hold fire
in bare hands—

The more I act upon it,
the more
charred
I get.

15. Loss

In her quest
to find someone
to fill the void
in her heart,

She never realized
how she lost herself—
irrevocably.

16. Melancholy

September—
you left me charred,
just like my past lover.

Oh, what a sin you committed—
bringing this huge little mane
swooping into my life,
only to take it away
with a flick of The Wand.

What conspired between

Time and Love?

A melancholy—
so holy
that the heavens bled
straight into the hell.
Blood so sacred,
flowing through despair—
an untimely union
of angels and demons.

An eternal fire
burning inside an abyss,
flames erupting
into a timeless symphony.

September—
you left me charred,
just like my past lover.

17. Longing

I held my hand out for you—
And you were there,
Running and spiraling,
Almost there.
Almost!

I could see how frantic you'd become,
So I held my hand out for you
Even further—
Literally pushing myself out of the train.
Almost there.
Almost!

Life was never a solo backpacking trip.
It has always been a roller coaster ride
Where we're meant to hold each other tightly,
As we scream with fear and thrill.

So I held my hand out for you.
I could see the creases on your palm,
The fear in your eyes,
The desperation in the way you moved—
As if all you ever wanted
Was to reach out.

Almost there.
Almost!

So I held my hand out for you,
For as long as I could,
For as long as you would.
I could see the way your body moved—
The momentary pause,
And then the shift of pace,
The wavering steps,
Slowing... and slowing...
Almost there.
Almost!

So I held my hand out for you
As the engine whistled,
And the distance between us grew longer.
As you slowly—but surely—stopped trying.

Tears rolled down my eyes
As your hand almost reached mine.
Almost there.
Almost!

But it didn't.

And just like that,
I could see you—
Getting smaller and smaller,
Until all you were
Was a tiny little blur.

A blur of the memories
We almost had.
A blur of the life
We almost shared.
Almost there.
Almost!

And then we were gone—
So far gone,
Leaving behind nothing
But all the haunting almosts
We almost had.

I closed my eyes
And almost saw you.

So I held my hand out for you,
As your hand reached for my face
And mine for yours...

Life hit me so hard

As I opened my eyes—
And you weren't really there.

But you almost were.
Almost there.
Almost.

18. Courage

I desperately cling to *us*
as the final remnants of love
slip through our fingers—
into the abyss,
into nothingness.

I look up at you,
into those bright brown eyes of yours—
and I see not love,
but fear.
Fear of loneliness.

And I know—
it's time to loosen my grip,
time to finally let go.

As I try to walk away,
you hold on still,
begging me to stay.
But tell me, my darling—
how can we live
in this loveless cage?
Bound not by love,
but by the fear of being alone?

As love finally fades,
I step over the edge,
climbing out of the abyss
into a bright, blinding world.

Should I look back?

My body wars with my mind,
fighting to keep walking
without turning around.
But when I do—
there you are,
still stuck in the cage,
clinging to the leftovers
of what we once had.

The war inside me burns
as I hold my ground,
resisting the pull
to run back into that hole of fear.

I cast one last glance at you—
begging you to let go.
There is nothing left
but darkness behind us,
waiting to consume us whole

if we return.

I take the reins of my life
into my own hands.
I tear the fear from my chest
and throw it far,
far away—
where it can never
crawl back.

And I turn.
And I walk away.
Once and for all.

Not turning back.
Not once.
Not once.

19. Separation

Have you ever felt so certain—
That your very existence
Was meant to love just one person?
That they were born only to become yours,
One day?

Have these feelings ever made perfect sense to you?
Or have you not been fortunate enough
To experience this kind of love?

Imagine falling head over heels
In love with that one person
Who truly meant it when they said they loved you...
Imagine falling in love with someone
Who loved you back just as much—
Probably even more.

Fairytale?
Seems like it, doesn't it?

Well...

Then imagine spending a decade of your life with them...

And then—
Imagine leaving all that behind.

Imagine waking up one day
And your phone doesn't have a good morning text from
them...
Imagine not falling asleep
While talking to them on a call.

How weird are the twists of fate!

One day you're in this cocoon
That's going to turn into a butterfly—
And the next, you're in this abyss,
This unending hollow
That reaches up to the horizon...

And you're drowning.
Drowning deeper and deeper
Each passing second.

Imagine them not being there
To hold your hand—
To steady you and say it's okay,
To hug you
And make you forget the whole world.

Imagine the world and everything in it pricking you...
Every living and non-living thing—
Made up of thorns, of needles—
Piercing your skin
And your soul.

Imagine them crying along with you,
Asking this again and again—
Why can't we be together?

Imagine you not being able to answer.
Imagine their heart breaking into a million pieces
because of you.
Imagine yours breaking into a gazillion ones...

Imagine touching them...
Not romantically—
Just imagine being able to touch them.
Reminisce that privilege.

Imagine you forgetting
The way their skin feels on yours.
Imagine never experiencing that touch again.
Imagine them kissing you on your forehead.
Imagine having to live without them.

What would life be—
Without the singular person
Whom you gave your entire being to?

Imagine dying a thousand deaths every day...
The fact that you're both completely broken,
Unable to exist without each other—
Yet imagine having to do so.

Imagine being in such a mental state
That you aren't happy with them...
And you both don't know happiness without each other.

Imagine a thousand beautiful things.
Imagine us together.

At least in our dreams, let us be one.
At least in another world, let us hold on to each other
And never leave.
At least in some parallel reality,
Our fingers are entwined now.

At least in death, reunite us.
At least let us be together in the afterlife.
At least let us be in love.

If not in this world—

At least let us be
In every other world,
Every other universe,
Every other reality.

At least give us that.
At least let all the yous and mes be united in love,
Happy and together
Until death does them apart.

We sacrificed our love
In this world...
Let it be worth it
In all the others.

Please...
Imagine—
And let us be...

In love...

In all the realities and all the dimensions.
All but this.
All... but this.

Let us be in love.

20. Nostalgia

Once, there was a boy who believed in love and destiny,
Who believed in miracles and loving someone endlessly.

Once, there was a boy who fell in love with the wrong
girl,
Who kept falling again and again,
Like a never-ending swirl.

Once, there was a boy, wounded so deeply and barely
alive.
He got cuts in his flesh, in his heart —
His mind struggled to survive.

Once, there was a boy who had hope, who had faith,
Then that fate was shattered,
Buried beneath love's wraith.

Once, there was a boy who loved a girl with all his heart.
In every minute of every day,
Never wanting to part.
He chose her above all, come what may,
At every turn, on every crossway.

Once, there was a boy who didn't know her love would
fade.
He kept trying and crying —
In pain, he stayed.

He asked for help,
But no one came.
Only silence answered
When he called her name.

Once, there was a boy she left like stone.
At life's crossroads, he stood all alone.
He wandered lost, with no guide in sight,
Swallowed by sorrow,
Stripped of light.

Once, there was a boy who was given a chance to heal,
Who was so immersed in darkness,
He pondered how sunshine would feel.

Once, there was a boy buried deep within,
Trapped in grief,
Too tired to begin.
He struggled to rise, to feel, to trust —
When all he touched
Turned back to dust.

Once, there was a boy
Whose wings were torn.
He forgot to fly, too weary, too worn.
When he tried to soar through the sky
With his mended wings,
He could barely fly.

Once, there was a girl who loved this boy,
Who longed to bring him
Light and joy.
To heal, protect, and stand beside,
To walk with him
Through every tide.

Once, there was a girl whose paths all led
To this boy, where her heart was fed.
She loved him deeply, night and day,
Though he kept drifting
Further away.

Once, there was a girl who dreamed her tale —
That love would bloom,
Would prevail.
She hoped he'd turn and take her hand,
Together, forever —
They'd bravely stand.

Once, there was a girl who longed to save,
To be the knight —
Bold and brave.
She dreamed of him, her prince so near,
Who'd ride through storms
And make all clear.

Once, there was a girl who kept on dreaming,
Lost in love,
Her soul still gleaming.
She gave her heart, but it was never returned —
And in that silence,
Her passion burned...

Once, there were a boy and a girl,
Entwined in fate's
Twisted whirl.
He with his wings, barely mended,
She with her love,
Fiercely extended.

She tried to lift him, but he stayed low.
He tried to reach her,
But couldn't go.

Once, there were a girl and a boy,
Whom fate did not bind together,

Who loved one another, but couldn't hold one another...

Once, there were a girl and a boy,
Who couldn't stay together.
It wasn't their time, it wasn't their world —
They belonged in the fairy tale,
Not in the real world.

Once, there were a boy and a girl,
Crossroads bound
In a cosmic swirl.
Drawn together, yet pulled apart —
Both carrying fragments
Of a shattered heart.

They hoped, one day, their roads would meet,
Where past and future
Could finally greet.
Where they'd no longer walk alone,
But build a life,
A love, a home.

Once, there were a boy and a girl,
Stuck in the mess of their own creation.
Hoping to attain some salvation,
Losing their prime,
Waiting still, throughout the history of time.

21. Liberation

September ended
with the beginning of autumn
in my life.

All the masks fell off
like dried leaves—
people stripped naked,
out from the illusions
that latched onto them.

Like the stems come undone—
raw and brown.

After the spring
there comes summer.
But autumn came uninvited.
It ran and barged through the doors,
kicking summer aside,
like it meant nothing
to skip seasons.

The autumn of my life
came on a Sunday afternoon.

Autumn didn't bother
to gently remove the leaves
from my body
with its bare hands.
Instead, it led me
through storms and tides.
Winds came gushing—
and snatched away my leaves.

Left me bare.
Brown.
Just like the naked stems.

I wanted to go
and hug all the trees in the universe—
for I felt their pain.
For autumn peeled away my skin too,
so mercilessly.

Autumn promised me winter.
But I always knew—
winter was coming.

All I wanted
was to soak in the sun,
bathe in the warmth,
until it seeped inside me

and became a part of me.

But autumn took away my summer.
The promised winter
came too soon.

Bare and brown—
I still couldn't bloom.

Is this how fast
the seasons always change?
Is this how autumn always comes?
To strip you naked?

Is the cover of snow
that winter brings—
a curse,
or a boon?

Is winter protecting me?
Laying fresh white snow
over my now brown wounds—

(Where was it
when I was bleeding?)

Or is it trying
to mask my stems?
Hiding away all the ugliness
they hold within?

Why does winter
come with the burden
of the snow cover?

After shedding away
every last weight,
winter brings a fresh batch
of a new white weight.

Winter came undone over me.
Fell from the sky—
straight atop.
Chilling my spine.

Now I weigh
more than I did.
This weight?
It's heavy.

A beautiful tragedy
has befallen me—
and I'm drowning now,

on the land,
underneath the snow.

Spring, are you listening?
Where are you?
It's been long due.
Come meet me soon.

Let me bask again
in the sunlight.
Let me bloom.

I want to witness
colours again.
I have turned too dark
to embrace the white now.

Please—
come bearing the yellow and the orange,
the blue and the red.
Bring violet and purple
along as well.

Let's make flowers together.
Let's yield fruits once again.

O Spring, I am waiting.
You are coming, right?
I'm counting on you.

After the unraveling...

- a love letter from the end, to the beginning

Hey,
Thank you for making it to the very end.
For staying—especially when it would've been easier to turn away.
It takes a rare kind of courage, more than most can ever comprehend, to stay despite of all the avalanches stirred inside you.

I didn't write this book to offer answers,
or to untangle the threads of the spells love casts.
I wrote it to say—
Me too.

I know the weight of what's left behind when love slips through your fingers.

I know the ache of almosts, the quiet of after.
The way grief takes up residence in corners you once
filled with hope.

But after the unraveling,
I hope something soft settled inside you:
That love was never really about the other.
It was always about finding your way back to yourself.

Every heartbreak, every silence,
was sculpting you into something celestial.

You carried longing like it was stitched into your skin,
bled stars into the night,
offered your heart like prayer—
only to discover:
you were never separate from the sacred.
You were the temple.
You were the flame.

The fairy tale was never a place to arrive.
It was the becoming,
written in each breath, each surrender.

Now, you no longer seek the spell.
You are the enchantment.
You no longer ask to be held—
you are your own sanctuary.

From the ashes,
you don't just rise—
you glow.
A memory of the stars,
returning home to themselves.

And this time,
you no longer hope for love to stay.
You become the love that never leaves.
You are not a chapter left unfinished.
You are the fairy tale,
spiraling into beginnings that never truly end.

You are myth.
You are the marrow of truth.
You're the silence and the song.
You're the light and the dawn.
You are the home you've been searching for all along.

Because you—
you are the beginning,
the becoming,
and the beyond.

*You thought love would
arrive from outside.*

*But all along,
it was quietly growing roots
in your soul.*

- Apoorvaa